Transformation

PAUL CHENEOUR

Redgoldmusic.com

Contents

Transformation vii
Dedication ix

TRANSFORMATION

About The Author 28

Transformation

Copyright © 2023 by Paul Cheneour

All rights reserved. No part of this book may be reproduced in any manner whatsoever without written permission except in the case of brief quotations embodied in critical articles and reviews.

First Printing, 2023

To those on the
path

Transformation

Nothing stays the same
The good
The bad
The indifferent
These too
Will fade soon enough
Change is the only constant
Do not cling
To ideas or things
Every event has its time
Of fruition and decay
Celebrate these moments
Of movement

Wheels within wheels
Always turning
Always spinning
Moving through cycles
Of pain
Of grief
Of anguish
Of compassion
Of kindness
Of ecstatic bliss
Keep true to your path
Turn as the sun and the moon turn

What would you like for breakfast
A bowl of mixed metaphors
A side order of palindromes
A tea laced with anachronistic tendencies
Oh yes and two scorched earths on toast
Washed down with a glass of fruitlessness
That and side order of irony
Will do nicely

Be a coherent human being
Be in balance with your Self
Be in balance with nature
Find your natural flowingness
Leave ideas of
More
Bigger
Better behind
Be strong in this life
Be supple like water
Follow the path of least resistance

In this silent house
Looking softly across the room
We are drowning in each other
The cracked mirror watches us
Beyond the certainty of opposites
Where sorrow and literalism ends
Laying down in this garden
We bathe in radiant sunlight
Of hot summers musings

In this time of truth decay
Resist the urge to label yourself
Be the point of your own attention
You are the one that needs change
Be that change you are seeking
Let the layers of illusion fall away
Forget that arguing nonsense
Become a moth
To the flame of knowing

Create emotional time markers
Feel the life force within
Stand vigorously still
For a moment
Remember how it feels
File it in your life memory
Do this often
Do this for the rest of your life

Stop being clever
Listen to your heart
Watch time passing
The opposite of life
Is not death
It is habit
What more is there to know

Do what you love doing
In right relationship
Then your life
Will flow to you

Sharing is the answer
Embrace cooperation
Banish competitiveness
Share no matter the cost
Work together
Be in each other
Be of each other
Be in unity

Change moves you forward
Leave your fears at the threshold
Walk calmly towards new truth
Old ideas are consigned to history
Embrace this never ending change

Stickleback Shrimp
Watermelon Apricot
Walnut Cashew
Elephant Hyena
Anteater Sloth
Lemon and Toad
Riding waves of time
On the wall mounted clock

A dark winter is approaching
Financial resets are looming
Insidious ideologies
Are salivating
At the thought of
Population control
Keep your mental footwork nimble
Maintain the two meter distance
Between yourself
And those who seek to
Enslave you

Turn off and tune in
Your path will be revealed
Stop clutching at those
Material centric views
The process towards intuition
Will unfold at the right time
It is flowing through us
Move within and dance
The ecstatic Dervish dance
Become the conscious intermediary
Between spirit and the material

There is no turning back
A new year has arrived
That voice in your head
Moves from
Affirming
Denying
To reconciling
In this emergence
Thoughts and actions
Have deep consequences
Review your intentions
Throw off sham connections
Begin healing
In gratitude

Arriving by stealth
A fading light shimmers
Almost unnoticed
Harvesting possibilities
Of what might be
Wrapped in a cool blanket
Of forgetfulness
We merge with the unseen world
Where feet tread so lightly
No grain of sand is disturbed
Do not forget that single note
From whence you came
Keep your ears open
And listen intently
For that beaconing sound

Come sit with me
For an eternal moment
Under this knowing tree

Eyes searching
Looking outward
My focus of attention
Wanders past the window pane
Towards imagination
Resting for a brief moment
On the tree line across the valley
What is it
I think I see

Today a gentle stillness cradles us
Tomorrow a relentless storm will arrive

Sparkling thoughts
Falling like rain drops
Splatter the ground
My inside is outside
My upside is down
My downside is up
Seagulls do their worm dancing
On the headstone of my grave

People shout and scream for
Prosecution and punishment
For thieves that steal
Now you are asked to vote for
Thieves who would steal your liberty
Do you see the irony in that

It is a glorious day
When you can finally say
I know that
I do not know

Walk towards emptiness
Question everything
Accept nothing but yourself
When you reach the abyss
Leave fears behind and fly
Love will carry you upwards
Words are useless at
Describing this Love
And only bring tears of frustration
Do not grieve when I am gone
My death ending is a coming together
Of a single drop of water
And the ocean

Today I feel a new sensation
Like floating ten feet
Above the ground
Tethered by a silver thread
This lightness is full of excitement
Like a cup being filled
With the heat of the sun

Catching a glimmer of truth
In everything you do
No matter the circumstances
Do not be fooled into accepting
Lies for truth
Measure what is being said
And demanded of you
Test it against your own reality
Is what you know
Still true

Seduction in its myriad forms
Can be deliciously tasty
But is it a sugar coated poison
Designed for entrapment
Learn discernment
Become aware
Know your true self
Side step those pitfalls
And see those temptations
For what they really are
Even pleasure is an illusion

Why struggle for recognition
Status and importance
To be picked out of the crowd
Needing special attention
What made you so anxious
Where did this crazy behaviour
For fighting so hard come from
Quieten your fears
Become as light as a feather
And truly sane again

Step away from the car sir
How often have you heard this
Someone is fearing your reaction
Demanding your submission
Someone is draining your energy
Resist that insane demand
Remember you are infinite
With strength power and free will
In this crazy third dimensional world

The system is insane
Not fit for purpose
In the face of hopelessness
Remain hopeful for a change

A lush green meadow
Comes alive
Where beauty and tranquillity
Stretch out beyond imagination
Perfectly balanced
Let us be together there
For an eternity

As we move towards the heart
Together we can
Search for mutual sustainability
Make a decision this moment
And turn away from
Mutually assured destruction

In a recent dream
The devil appeared
Taunting me saying
Is that all you have
Just weak breath
And no fire
You cannot fight me
Little human
Listen devil I said
I will succeed
I have bountiful love
And am a spark of the divine

Sing your songs
For a six pence
With pockets full of rye
The folks in this town
Hide behind
Closed eyes

Walk in silver time
Nature spirits sprinkle their
Happy talk about ending sorrows
Oppose deception
Oppose bondage
Meet us at the rainbow windmill
Even if you feel world weary
Join the growing awakening

This time thing is precious
Use it wisely
In your brief life sojourn
Make wise choices
Work together and share
Greet each day a new
Revel in your struggles
Grow and become more you

Your existence
Is but a fleeting moment
In the great scheme of things
Each moment confined here
On this earthly plane is
Polishing you for greatness
And sparkling perfection

In spring
Forests turn
From brown
To green

Be quiet I said
Make a sound like an ant
Two three four
Stamp
Crash
Bang
Wallop
An ant with army boots

The new human
Is an integration
Of physicality
Energy and light
Prepare yourselves
For bonding
And transition

Images of deserts
Irrigate imaginations
Drenched bodies swathed
In clinging humid heat
Limpets scurry for shelter
Peace finally descends
On a troubled heart

Why
Do we
Why do we not
Talk
Do we not talk
Anymore
Why do we not talk anymore
Why

Fire cleans the body
Softened
By the intermediary
Of Water

A sunbeam surprised me
With its delicious embrace
Directly from the ancestral home
Reminding me of the nearness of you

Sieve your emotional soil
Thoroughly
Even in late spring
Begin sowing seeds
Of wisdom

Grey robed zen monks
Breakfasting at café Brenda
Cooking up new recipes
Dancing in line together
A new fraternity awakens
Transition has begun
Feel the warmth
Feel the calm
Feel the pure delight
That comes from
Joined up thinking

Leave behind
Old ways
Old energies
Old paradigms
Embrace the new
Create a masterpiece
That is you

Shine a light on your path
It will twist and turn
No wrong or right ways
Expect the unexpected
Free from illusion
And thinking of others
Leave dogmatic philosophy
And theology behind
Trust your Self to be the guide
To return you home

Let experience
Be your guide
Revaluate perceptions
Great truths
Are being revealed
Break your heart open
Be alert to otherness

Each moment of existence
Is charged with possibilities
Align your etheric bodies
Balance your manifested layers
New probabilities will emerge
Embrace the unfolding
Let your heart lead you
In that direction
Your path is being elevated

Move away from theisms
Source is indifferent
To your pleading
You alone decide paths
Of joy
Or suffering
Of becoming a real
Human being
Quench your thirst
For true understanding
With the wine that is
Your Life

Rhythm is a division of time
Do not waste this precious gift
On trivial pursuits
Explore your inner universe
Discover your innate wisdom
Beat the knowing drum in tempo
Turn in divine ecstasy

Seek clarity and perfection
Seek authenticity
Seek ecstatic joy
Become one with all things
Beyond the boundaries of sensation
Hear that sacred sound and
Resonate in wild abandonment

In the heart garden
Plant wonderous seeds
Of glorious possibilities

Wounded from indifference and betrayal
Limping towards a thoughtful tenderness
See through the tears of pain
In this endless trial of
What is mine and
What is not mine
Take courage oh heart
The end of sorrows is near
Closer than you can imagine
Trust in the order of things
Everything is as it is
And as it should be
All is in order
Although difficult to understand
In the midst of suffering

Can you hear
My heart singing
From the rooftops
Delirious with gratitude
For tearing me open

How many times
Does a heart need to break
Before it is broken open
This path towards yourself
Will be filled with pitfalls
Littered with agonies
Full of grief and despair
But leading to an ecstasy
Beyond comparison
Filling you with an
Unimaginable vitality
And knowingness

Do not be against something
Your energy will only give it strength
And will defeat you
Be resistance through joy
Be resistance through art
Be resistance through trust
Be resistance through love
Create the change inside you
Then outward manifestation
Will follow as sure as day
Follows night

Worry and despair are transformed
By an undefeated heart
Dissolve into compassion
Leave all worries by the door
Do not be trapped by preconceptions
About what should or should not be
Forget about judging
Make things as right as you can
Give up addictive thinking and take action
Beauty can only save the world
Let your heart decide what matters

Daily struggles
Lead us down empty paths
Do not be caught
In obsessions because
Love will fly out of the window
Waiting to be called again
If you forget loving
You will shrivel and wither
Time to begin loving again
When a new day arrives

Last night the moon came
Softly caressing this cheek
With tender kisses of forgiveness
Saying I stand in perfect balance
Between ending and beginning
Then I moved forward
With new courage
Towards a beautiful
Unknown

In a time of remembering
Old ideas and attitudes soften
Forget about making a profit
There is a light shining
So brightly inside you
If you could only see it
Turn towards what you love
Ask to see the truth of it
And the truth of yourself

Do not fear destruction
Of an idea
A building
An edifice
A system
A better way will arrive
From inspired thinking
Destruction brings renewal
Sufis say
Die to your Self
And see with new eyes
With a new heart
Be in the world
But not of it

A smiling laconic mouth appears
Glistening with sculptured white teeth
Scattering sweetly chosen words
Wrapped with enticing intentions
Demanding an enthusiastic endorsement
About beliefs and dubious ideas
Be alert to odious deceptions
From peddlers of snake oil remedies

Displacement
Moving from one condition to another
Moving from one place to another
Moving from one form to another
Moving from one idea to another
Always moving towards liberation

There is a soul science
Waiting in the wings
For consciousness
To open into this newness
Waiting for the right time
Is this the moment
Is this the right time
Yes

Energy precedes
Form and matter
Substance flows
From thought to matter

Life unfolds as it should
Cleanse emotions
Dissipate fears
Arrive at clarity
Be like Zhuangzi
The sage of uncertainty

Know you are a life entity
Creating a new earth
Speak to everything
Take part in the conversation
With plants
With the trees
With animals
Let life flow through you
And turn again in ecstasy

Embrace the beautiful paradox
That you are
An enormous sovereign being
And an insignificant irrelevance
At the same time
Let it percolate
Through your being
Until a bright luminosity
Bursts through
From your centre

Release yourself
From the prison
Of predictability
Remain in a state
Of permanent transition
Dissolve into
Ultimate knowing

Paul Cheneour has walked a broader musical path throughout his career embracing European Classical, Jazz, Arab, Indian, Celtic, and other music's, culminating in his own 'World Fusion' style.

"Tapping into the source of creativity takes great courage and even greater competence in acquired skills.

Paul Cheneour, a leading UK jazz, classical and ethnic flautist/composer suffered a near fatal car crash in '91.

He recovered with the conviction that he needed to use his talent, life, and near-death experience to explore a new forms of creative expression. This amounts to an opening out to the influences available in the moment.

All the world's great musical and artistic traditions remain as resources and are no longer seen as restrictive boundaries"

(Interview extract by Michael Greevis for Colour Therapy Magazine UK. 1995)

www.ingramcontent.com/pod-product-compliance
Lightning Source LLC
Chambersburg PA
CBHW021134080526
44587CB00012B/1290